KEN

METALCRAFTS
OF CENTRAL ASIA

SHIRE ETHNOGRAPHY

Cover photograph
A brass plaque worked in repoussé and chasing; Mongolian People's Republic.
A Buddhist guardian deity decorates this modern ornamental plaque made for
local use and the tourist market. Diameter 12 cm.

British Library Cataloguing in Publication Data:
Teague, Ken.
Metalcrafts of Central Asia. — (Shire ethnography; 19).
1. Asian metalware.
I. Title.
739.095.
ISBN 0-7478-0062-6.

Published by
SHIRE PUBLICATIONS LTD
Cromwell House, Church Street, Princes Risborough,
Buckinghamshire HP17 9AJ, UK.

ISBN 0 7478 0062 6

First published 1990.

Printed in Great Britain by
C. I. Thomas and Sons (Haverfordwest) Ltd,
Press Buildings, Merlins Bridge, Haverfordwest, Dyfed.

Contents

Acknowledgements

I am grateful to Mike Hitchcock and Jane Wilkinson who made many helpful suggestions about this book, and especially to my wife for her help and encouragement. I wish to thank the Trustees of the British Museum for their kind permission to publish photographs of their collections; also the staff of the Society for Cultural Relations with the USSR and of the museums which gave permission to publish many of the illustrations: the Horniman Museum, London; the Museum of Mankind, London; the Pitt Rivers Museum, Oxford; the Whitworth Art Gallery, Manchester. Where not otherwise stated, the illustrations are the author's copyright.

4

List of illustrations

1
Introduction

In central Asia the use of metals has been a major factor in the development of the various societies of the region. Whilst cities were the main centres of production, nomadic peoples played a part in transmitting metal technology and usage across central Asia, between China and the West.

Several influences are expressed in the metalcrafts of central Asia, deriving from the bordering civilisations of Iran, India and China, as well as from major religions including Buddhism and Islam. The Animal style, based on the depiction of animals in distorted postures, was a feature of nomadic metal artefacts. While China has had the longest single influence, Russian expansion into central Asia has had major effects on material culture and ethnography.

Contemporary craftsmen continue to use traditional and modern forms and motifs in their production of goods for local markets and to meet the increasing demand from tourists.

Geography

Central or Inner Asia is the region between the Caspian Sea and western Manchuria, which is bounded by China, India, Iran and Siberia. The region consists of the central Asian republics of the USSR, namely Kazakhstan, Tadzhikistan, Turkmenistan, Kirghizia and Uzbekistan (all sometimes called Russian Turkestan), and southern Siberia; northern Iran and Afghanistan; the north and west of China — Xinjiang (sometimes called Chinese Turkestan) and Inner Mongolia; Tibet and the Mongolian People's Republic (Outer Mongolia). Present political boundaries are misleading in encompassing this distinctive region.

Central Asia has a variety of ecological zones ranging from mountains and high plateaux to forests, steppes or prairie lands, scrub and deserts.

The climate is generally arid and continental with extreme shifts of temperature. Seasonal droughts are a recurring problem. Some desert areas support little plant life. Others, including the Gobi, support scrub vegetation which allows the pasturing of large herds of animals. In contrast, oasis regions, based on the rivers and streams running from melting mountain snows, may be several hundreds of square miles in area.

Before the development of modern transport, travel across

1. Map of central Asia.

central Asia was a lengthy process. In 1271 Marco Polo started on his journey from Venice to the court of Kubilai Khan and took over three years to reach Beijing. Earlier, in 1246, Friar John of Plano Carpini visited the Mongol empire on behalf of Pope Innocent IV. The Mongols decided that the friar should attend the coronation of their new Khan, Guyuk, and hurried him from their base camp on the Volga across central Asia to their capital at Karakorum to witness the ceremony. By using five or six relays of horses per day this journey of 3000 miles (4800 km) was accomplished in three and a half months.

Today the Trans-Siberian and the Turk-Siberian railways traverse central Asia in a few days, whilst airlines and motor transport criss-cross the region serving both the local population and tourists.

Peoples of central Asia

The ethnic mixture of the peoples of central Asia reflects the repeated movements of two basic stocks, Indo-Europeans from the west and Turkic-Mongols from the east. Frequent migrations, conquests and resettlement have resulted in a mosaic of societies and cultures.

From about AD 750 to 1750 Turkic and Mongol peoples were politically dominant, and the region was one where large empires were repeatedly established, only to decline. In more recent centuries the basic populations in the cities and villages have been Iranians and Chinese, with some settled nomadic groups such as the Uighurs in Xinjiang, and the Uzbeks in Uzbekistan. In the rural areas the people are mostly Turkish or Mongol.

The nomadic peoples are known today as Kazakh, Kirghiz, Uzbek, Turkmen and Mongols. These peoples, originally from the Altai region and Mongolia to the east, have been given various names over the centuries. The Chinese have termed them Yue Chi ('tent dwellers'), Hsiung Nu ('Huns') and Tu Gyu ('Turks').

The earliest records of mounted nomads in Western sources are Assyrian, from about 700 BC, when the first bands of Scythians were encountered. In the Bible they are called the people of Gog and Magog. Their lifestyle was recorded by Greek historians such as Herodotus. In the wake of the Mongol invasions of eastern Europe in the thirteenth century Louis IX of France termed them 'Tartars', or denizens of *Tartaros,* hell.

At times these peoples have spread far outside the boundaries of central Asia proper, the Scythians to southern Russia, the Huns to Hungary. The Mongols under Genghis Khan established an enormous empire from eastern Europe to the Pacific. In the words of a contemporary in about 1253, 'The Tartars have divided among themselves Scythia, which stretches from the Danube as far as the rising of the sun.'

The Turkic peoples also settled on the Eurasian borderlands, founding dynasties which ruled Iran and Turkey into the twentieth century.

2. Salimdjan Khamidov, a notable metal craftsman of Bukhara, Uzbek SSR. (Society for Cultural Relations with the USSR.)

2
Metalcrafts and society

Since the neolithic revolution the societies of central Asia have been based on two main forms of subsistence: irrigation agriculture in the oases and along the river valleys; and nomadic pastoralism (the moving of herds of livestock to fresh pastures and water supplies) in areas outside the oases where crop growth is sparse. Archaeological evidence shows that simple irrigation agriculture and stock-breeding were practised from about 6000 to 5000 BC in western central Asia, south of the Aral Sea. Copper implements were in use from about 4000 BC.

Urban life

Towns, in contact with Mesopotamia and the Indus valley, developed from about 3000 to 1500 BC. From about 1000 BC some developed into great cities with complex social organisations. Samarkand and Bukhara, amongst others, were centres of culture and controlled the trade routes crossing the region. The ruler and aristocracy governed a subject peasantry and a number of merchants and craftsmen with the aid of an army. At times a dynasty would establish an empire consisting of a number of cities, estates and settlements.

Foreign merchants and travellers brought in ideas and beliefs, supplementing indigenous religions. Islam was, and still is, the major cultural influence in oasis society in western central Asia and Xinjiang, whilst Buddhism was the primary influence in Tibet and Mongolia until the twentieth century.

Metalcrafts in central Asia developed to meet the demands of the urban and nomadic aristocracy, then later for the monasteries of Buddhism and the mosques of Islam and for the ordinary people, either for local consumption or for trade. Production for some or all of these markets continued into the twentieth century.

Urban craftsmen produced for urban and rural populations, both settled and nomad, and have always dominated production in central Asia, where the cities have been centres of innovation in styles and technology in craftwork, especially from workshops under court patronage.

The typical urban arrangement persisted into the twentieth century in cities such as Bukhara and Kashgar. A town consisted of two parts: a walled area containing the ruler's palace and

3. (Left) The former summer palace of the Emir of Bukhara is now a museum; Bukhara, Uzbek SSR. (Society for Cultural Relations with the USSR.)

4. (Right) A Buddhist street shrine and the Maidar temple, Ulan Bator, Mongolian People's Republic. The temple, unopened for many years, contains a gilded copper figure of Maidar (Maitreya), the future Buddha, which is 16 metres high.

administrative buildings, with quarters for the aristocracy and craftsmen working for the court; and outside this the bazaar area, also walled, containing suburbs, trading places and more craft workshops, often arranged into quarters according to different crafts.

Towns and cities depended for their wealth on trade and agricultural produce from the surrounding countryside. Goods were also imported from long distances, so the material culture of central Asia shows influences from many of the surrounding regions of Asia and has in turn influenced them. All the major cities produced metal wares, and each had a catchment area for its products.

Because the records are poor it is not easy to determine how many craftsmen there were, but it has been estimated that in Bukhara there were about 150 smiths in 1850, and about 400 in 1900. Nor is it easy to establish the ethnic grouping of urban metalworkers. In modern literature they are often called 'Sarts', but this term is applied also to Tadzhiks, 'non-Turks' (either free or enslaved) from Iran, as well as to settled Uzbek, Kirghiz and

Kazakh nomads. In the middle ages the Arabs employed central Asian metalworkers, who for centuries had had a reputation for fine work, as well as captured Chinese craftsmen.

Since some workshops depended on patronage for their livelihood, craftsmen might be required to move great distances, at the wish of their patrons, thereby spreading their ideas and skills.

Metal craftsmen were and are organised in groups. In some cases these groups were formed as guilds, for example in Uzbekistan before 1920 and in Afghanistan more recently. Metalworkers' guilds had statutes, precepts, legends of origin and a prophet or saint as a patron who was invoked during smelting and casting. King David is the legendary patron of all Muslim metalworkers and is thought to be buried in northern Afghanistan.

The wives and children of craftsmen helped in production, and a craftsman's children inherited the occupation. A craftsman who had gained a reputation for artistry might be commissioned to produce metalwares by the wealthy. Objects were also given to mosques as acts of charity.

Craft workshops often had marked divisions of specialisation in designing, casting and shaping metal, and decoration. Within the group different craftsmen specialised in making different parts of vessels, soldering the parts together, or decorating completed metalwares. Traditional techniques are still used today, and some cities are famous for particular techniques: Bukhara for enamel, cloisonné and niello, and Khiva for filigree decoration.

Craftsmen to great households and monasteries

In Tibet and Mongolia the Buddhist monasteries and the households of great lords provided markets and employment for local artisans as well as for craftsmen from external regions. Newari metal craftsmen from Nepal were widely used in Tibet and China from the thirteenth century until present times. Chinese craftsmen produced goods for Mongolian princes and Tibetan monasteries from their workshops in the towns of Gansu and Inner Mongolia. The Khalkha Mongols also had their own craftsmen, probably trained in the monasteries, to produce religious artefacts.

About 1900 there was some specialisation of craft products in different cities in Tibet: most silversmiths worked in Shigatse, and most goldsmiths in Lhasa. It was generally recognised that the best workers in precious metals in Tibet were Newaris from

Nepal. Women were employed to work the bellows in the furnaces for melting metal in the Lhasa mint at this time. Lower-class Tibetans also worked in metal in Lhasa, as elsewhere in Tibet. Blacksmiths were regarded as outcastes, a common pattern in many parts of Asia.

Derge was the best metalworking centre in eastern Tibet until modern times. The earliest Chinese sources which note the metalworking skills of the Tibetans probably refer to this area. In Derge lamas of the Red Hat sects were involved in metalworking. Different monastic orders may also have produced their own types of religious images in different parts of the country. Although there is little written information on this topic, there are considerable numbers of Tibetan artefacts, especially metalwares, in museum collections.

Nomadic life

Central Asia is distinguished as the area of origin of nomadic tent-dwelling societies of herders whose main concern was, and is, raising livestock. After the development of pastoral nomadism as an extension of the mixed farming economy of settled peoples, mounted nomadism, using the horse as a riding animal, developed about 1000 to 900 BC on the western steppes and spread extremely rapidly across Asia.

5. (Left) Branding iron in Myangad Sum camp. (Copyright: K. Chabros.)

6. (Right) Herders' camp in western Mongolia, Myangad Sum, Xord Aimak. In the foreground a makeshift pen for young animals is made from parts of a tent. (Copyright: K. Chabros.)

The nomadic lifestyle in central Asia is based on herding a combination of livestock: sheep (predominantly), goats, horses and perhaps cattle and camels. In Tibet and other high-altitude areas yaks are the main form of livestock.

Mounted nomads are able to move far and fast. Their material culture, including their housing, is portable. Living in marginal lands where cultivation is not viable, nomads have often eluded the authority of town-based governments. Although usually a minority of the population, nomads could often mobilise an effective force of cavalry which enabled their leaders to conquer other nomadic groups and settled peoples, establishing dynastic rule over towns and controlling trade routes, before falling in turn before a new conquering force, itself often led by nomads.

Basic subsistence was traditionally based on the products of their herds, but while the nomadic peoples were often in conflict with their settled neighbours they were nevertheless dependent on them for commodities such as agricultural products and metalwares.

A nomadic lifestyle, with its need for mobility, inhibits the development of mining and the use of machinery to extract and work metals. In recent times nomads have usually been dependent on urban craftsmen or on a few itinerant craftsmen from either their own or neighbouring peoples. This has not always been so: mining, smelting and forging were all part of the nomadic lifestyle from its earliest development. The Turkic peoples from the Altai and the Tuvans were noted metalworkers.

It is said that craftsmen are often despised in nomadic cultures. However, smiths are generally respected and may have high social status in Mongolia. The Buriat Mongols regard smiths as divine in origin and the Khalkhas also venerate them. Many may be descendants of the craftsmen who were assembled during the establishment of the Mongol empire in the thirteenth century. The craft is passed down among the men of a family.

In the thirteenth century the Islamic world and eastern Europe were invaded by a new cultural force: the Mongols. Originally from the borders of Mongolia and Manchuria, the Mongols were united under Genghis Khan. During their campaigns throughout central Asia and as far as eastern Europe many craftsmen were captured and removed to serve the Mongol aristocracy.

The Mongol empire also fostered the spread of techniques and styles in metalworking and other arts and crafts between eastern and western Asia. In Karakorum craftsmen might be from very distant cultures. In 1253/4 William Rubruck, the Franciscan missionary, met a goldsmith from Paris who had been captured in Hungary and was now working at Mongke Khan's court. Iranian and Chinese craftsmen were forcibly resettled on a large scale in Mongolia and Siberia, where they mined and made tools and weapons for the Mongols. Genghis Khan favoured a class of Turkic craftsmen, and the title of *darkhan* or 'smith' was also applied to high-ranking officers in the Mongol army at this time. Elsewhere local craftsmen were not so lucky. The Mongols destroyed the Kirghiz state in the Minusinsk Basin. Irrigation agriculture was abandoned there, crafts decayed and the Kirghiz became illiterate.

One of the last peaks of nomadic power in central Asia was reached about 1400 when Tamerlaine or Timur established a huge empire with his capital at Samarkand. Craftsmen, artists and builders were forcibly assembled to render their services to the new ruler's short-lived civilisation.

Metalcrafts in recent times
After the Timurid dynasty Mongol and Turkic power in central Asia declined. One reason for this was the development of sea routes as alternatives to the land routes across Asia. In the west the Shia Muslim Iranians cut off western central Asia, one of the most important parts of the Muslim world, from the rest of Sunni Islam. Further north, the Russians under Ivan the Terrible defeated the remains of the Mongol/Tatar kingdoms on the western steppes in the sixteenth century and started to settle and cultivate this area on a permanent basis. Although the Uzbek empire based on Bukhara was briefly united, and agriculture, trade and crafts were fostered during the eighteenth and early nineteenth centuries, it disintegrated into small principalities. Trade and craft production declined further under persistent nomadic raiding of the caravans, the effects of the Russian conquest of central Asia and the import of Russian products.

In the eastern part of central Asia, a similar closure occurred. In the sixteenth and seventeenth centuries close ties were forged between Tibet and Mongolia. In 1578 the Abbot of Drepung in Tibet was entitled 'Dalai Lama' by Altan Khan, the most powerful Mongol lord. After this the Tibetans preached Buddhism in the Mongol lands on a large scale. Craftsmen became established in the monasteries which were built, especially in Inner Mongolia, where they produced religious figures and apparatus. Often however, especially in Inner Mongolia, Chinese craftsmen inhibited Mongolian development and fostered an increasing dependence on China. In modern times the Mongols have relied heavily on the products of Beijing and Chinese border towns for their metalwares and other products, although a noble household usually contained its own resident craftsmen. The nomadic Manchu dynasty ruling China encouraged the spread of Buddhism among the Mongols as a means of pacifying them. In 1691 the Manchus conquered Mongolia and closed its frontiers to foreigners, and in 1792 they closed Tibet also.

During the nineteenth century Russian expansion into central Asia continued, with Russian peasants being settled on the better lands of the conquered peoples. Meanwhile the British were intent on gaining commercial access to the region from India. After having been one of the major centres of economic, political and cultural activity in the world, central Asia was in decline.

From the late nineteenth century onwards the European powers, Britain, France and Germany, as well as Russia, the United States and Japan, sent a number of expeditions to central Asia to explore and carry out archaeological and botanical work. In 1904 the Younghusband Expedition entered Tibet by force, to establish commercial and political ties between Tibet and India. In 1907 Russia and Britain defined their spheres of interest in central Asia and guaranteed the independence of Afghanistan. The 'Great Game' was in full swing. It was during this period that much of the central Asian material present in museum collections was gathered.

In western central Asia metalcrafts declined following the Russian conquest and the building of the Caspian railway. The quality of urban jewellery deteriorated. Urban locksmiths turned to tinkering, as did blacksmiths and coppersmiths in the rural areas. Craftsmen who were highly skilled in casting jugs and cauldrons in non-ferrous metals turned to making iron plough-shares and wheel hubs because of increasing imports of raw materials and factory-made products from Russia and India. The gunsmiths of Fergana had a high reputation in the late nineteenth century but had mostly gone out of business by 1900, when even iron pots were imported from Russia although local craftsmen were still alive.

In Tuva, to the north-west of Mongolia, a well developed metalworking tradition suffered a similar decline due to increasing Russian influence. About 1900 there were more than five hundred blacksmiths in Tuva, mostly in the west, about one smith to every twenty or thirty households. Most smiths were not

jewellers (there were about seven or eight blacksmiths to one silversmith) but produced forged goods to order: pots, trivets,
rifles, tools and horse harness. Some iron ore was still extracted
but the main source of metal was old iron vessels and tools recast
into ingots, which were either provided by the customer or
bought by the smith from Chinese or Russian merchants. By the
1920s local craft products were superseded by Russian imported
goods: horse harness, trivets, other metalwares and jewellery.
Many smiths stopped making commissioned objects and by the
1950s mass settlement and collectivisation had reduced the
demand for local craft products in favour of manufactured goods.

After the Russian revolution in 1917, and the adoption of com-
munism in western central Asia, trade and mining were developed on an increasing scale in Kazakhstan, Uzbekistan and Fergana.

Industrialisation and the forced settlement and collectivisation
of the nomadic people were not easily accomplished. Thousands
of Kazakhs fled to Xinjiang and Afghanistan. Eventually policy
was revised and herding reinstated in the local economy of
western central Asia. The herds are now increasing again, even
though cultivation, mining and industry inevitably encroach on
pasture land. Today there is often a resident blacksmith at the
centre of a collective who maintains tools and implements and
makes traditional objects and jewellery to order.

Under socialism craftsmen in the USSR and the Mongolian
People's Republic are organised into co-operatives working to
demand under state patronage. From the 1950s onwards craft co-
operatives in the USSR were reorganised as state industries. In
Uzbekistan craftsmen serve a long apprenticeship working under
the direction of a master craftsman. Products in precious and
non-ferrous metals are made for local use and the tourist market.

Eastern central Asia has developed in a more fragmentary
fashion in the twentieth century. After the breakdown of Manchu
rule in China, both Mongolia and Tibet declared their independence in 1911. A Communist-led revolution in Outer Mongolia
resulted in the establishment of the Mongolian People's Republic
there. Pastoralism has been retained as the mainstay of the
economy but mining, industrialisation and agriculture have been
developed.

Mongolian metalwares have developed in different ways.
Inner Mongolia, which had the greater number of Buddhist monasteries, was colonised by Chinese peasants in the twentieth century. This reduced the traditional form of pastoral economy and

7. The metalworker Salimdjan Khamidov and his apprentices; Bukhara, Uzbek SSR. The USSR and Mongolia train new generations of craftsmen, both as apprentices to master craftsmen and in art schools. (Society for Cultural Relations with the USSR.)

created a dependence on Chinese craftsmen and products among the local population. Apart from the craft production of the Chinese border towns, itinerant craftsmen, both Chinese and Mongolian, worked among the nomadic communities of Mongolia. Here a craftsman might leave his own camp and settle elsewhere to produce metal artefacts, especially silverwares, to order. This was easily done since a smith's equipment was portable and a workshop might be set up in one part of a customer's tent without much disrupting household activities.

Whilst Inner Mongolia suffered from the effects of warfare and unrest after the Japanese invasion of China, Outer Mongolia maintained its independence and, after a communist revolution, became the Mongolian People's Republic in 1921. The Khalkha

Mongols have kept their metalworking traditions alive, with craftsmen making figures and silver jewellery especially. Today craftsmen often work in several media, decorating their products for local and tourist markets with Buddhist motifs and images. Copper is extensively used, notably for items such as tea bowls and ornaments in domestic and public contexts: the massive wall plaque, 6 by 2 metres, on the stairway of the Museum of the Revolution in Ulan Bator is a prime example. There is a thriving art school in the capital which is training younger craftsmen.

Xinjiang was much less developed than western Turkestan. Traditionally the region contained a sparse nomadic population and small oasis towns. Numerous tribal groups are present, with the Muslim Uighurs in the majority. Kashgar is the largest bazaar town. Coppersmiths, tinsmiths and jewellers work among other small manufacturing industries. Since the Second World War the Chinese have expanded into Xinjiang, developing the local economy and making it more sedentary. Wulumchi (Urumchi), the capital of Xinjiang, has been industrialising since 1949 and the region is a source of ferrous, non-ferrous and precious metal ores.

In Tibet, Derge metalwares declined in quality in the early part of the twentieth century and the nomads of the north-eastern borders became increasingly dependent on imported metalwares from India and China, including iron cooking pots, needles, sword-blades and firearms.

Tibet tried to retain its isolation and independence but was defeated by the Communist Chinese, who invaded in 1950. In 1959 there was an uprising and the Dalai Lama and some 100,000 Tibetans left to seek refuge in India and Nepal. During the Chinese Cultural Revolution, from 1966 to 1976, there was wholesale destruction of the Tibetan people and culture, with a decline in all traditional handicrafts. Since then the Chinese have developed the mineral resources of Tibet on a considerable scale and, from 1986, have tried to revive local handicrafts. Increasing tourism in Tibet, as in Xinjiang, has stimulated the demand for craft products and one may find antique jewellery and metal-wares, which must be certified for export, as well as an increasing number of fakes. In their efforts to maintain their culture in exile, Tibetan refugees have ensured that Tibetan metalwares and the products of several other crafts are more widely available. Some of the finest genuine Tibetan specimens may now be found in Kathmandu in Nepal, where there is an increasing production of metalwares for the tourist market, as there is in India.

3
Styles and decoration

The metalwares of central Asia show several distinctive stylistic influences. The Animal style, used by the nomadic peoples, probably represents indigenous sources and beliefs, with roots in shamanism and a regard for the powers and behaviour of animals. Other influences derive from China and Iran and from Buddhism and Islam, two major religions of external origin which were adopted in central Asia. The establishment of great empires such as those of the Mongols and the Timurids also resulted in the mixing of styles from much further afield. Ancient forms and motifs deriving from all of these sources still find expression in contemporary crafts.

Animal style

As nomadic societies based on stock-raising developed on the steppes between south Russia and Manchuria from about 1000 BC onwards, their culture found expression in an art style which used the natural forms of animals — stags, tigers, bears, boars and birds — in a reduced, contorted and stylised fashion. The forms were of real or fabulous animals, either whole or dismembered, with features such as horns used in a repetitive way. These animal motifs were expressed in several crafts including wood-carving and textiles as well as metalworking.

Metal objects decorated in this style include weapons, armour and horse harness (bridles, bits, saddles and stirrups). In earlier times chariot fittings and standards were also decorated in this way, along with belt plaques, strap ends, buckles and cauldron handles. The Animal style is still evident in contemporary articles, including eating utensils, prayer-wheels (figure 8) and decorative plaques (figure 9), from Buddhist countries which are now Communist such as Tibet and Mongolia.

Animal-style motifs are carved either flat or in low relief in rectangular or circular shape; less commonly they are found in the round as finials or handles.

The origins of Animal-style art are ascribed to various sources including China, southern Siberia, Tuva and the Altai as well as the Pontic Steppes north of the Black Sea. This style is also described as 'Scytho-Siberian' in an attempt to encompass the range of peoples who practised it. There are a number of common motifs.

8. (Left) Animal-style motif on a Buddhist prayer-wheel; Tibet, nineteenth century AD. This animal's head, *tao tieh,* was used as a motif on bronzes dating from the Shang Dynasty in China (1600-1027 BC). (Horniman Museum.)

9. (Right) Plaque, Mongolian People's Republic, showing an ibex in the Animal style. The method of indicating the animal's muscles is common to ancient Persia and southern Siberia. The stag, which was also a typical Scythian motif, is believed to carry the souls of the dead to the next world. This modern copper plaque is made for local and tourist use. Diameter: 23 cm. (Horniman Museum.)

The dragon, an ancient motif which probably derives from China about 1000 BC, has been popular throughout central Asia for centuries (figure 11). The dragon is depicted in various ways, including a circular form and as the frontal view of a monster's face, the *tao tieh,* which is represented on Chinese bronzes from 1000 BC and Tibetan prayer-wheels from AD 1900. In Muslim central Asia a dragon motif on a vessel is thought to protect the contents from contamination.

The stag with laid-back antlers and legs tucked under the body was a particular feature of Scythian art about 500-600 BC and later spread eastwards to the Altai and Siberia. Today a standing form is used in decorative metalwares from the Mongolian People's Republic.

Bird-of-prey motifs, often represented only by a head with a

10. Pair of silver ear ornaments with a double-headed bird inside the circle, a dot-and-circle motif in low relief and four fluted globules; the wire loops issue from the mouths of monsters; Turkmen, Iran. The double-headed bird motif is an ancient central Asian symbol which protects against evil. Diameter: 5 cm. (Horniman Museum.)

large eye and a long curved beak, may have developed either in China or the Altai and then passed westwards. In the form of a double-headed bird, possibly an eagle, or as wings this motif is used on metalwares in western Tibet and on jewellery from western central Asia.

Fabulous animal motifs other than the dragon appear to have been introduced into central Asia from Iran. These include griffins, horned eagles, winged bulls, some with human heads, and animals locked in combat. Composite creatures, including animals joined together, were a feature of Scythian art, whilst men with birds' heads are found on Iranian wares from the nineteenth century.

The lion as a motif came from Iran, where it symbolised the sun and power. Later it came to symbolise Buddha. In eastern central Asia tiger motifs were preferred.

Opposed pairs of animals derive from Iranian and other ancient cultures in the Near East and were popular in western central Asia. In the eastern areas there was a preference for coiled animal motifs.

Other animals often depicted in Animal style include wolves, ibex (China), mountain goats and sheep (Minusinsk), deer, elk (Pazyryk), elephants and horses, in addition to anecdotal scenes between humans (Kazakhstan). The spread of such motifs, along with forms and techniques, backwards and forwards across central Asia indicates the rapidity of communications which traditionally existed in this region. Few crafts arose and developed in isolation.

Animal style faded in central Asia after the introduction of Buddhism and later of Islam. Yet many of these motifs are still expressed, often in highly abstract or fragmentary form, in the artefacts of the region today.

11. (Left) Tinned brass ewer with a dragon motif around the base of the spout; Kashgar, Xinjiang. The dragon is an ancient motif which has been popular across central Asia from China to western Asia. Height: 43 cm. (Horniman Museum.)

12. (Right) Avalokitesvara or Chenresig; brass and copper; eastern Tibet; nineteenth century AD. The Dalai Lama is regarded as the incarnation of this Bodhisattva of Compassion. Height: 61 cm. (Horniman Museum.)

Buddhist style

Buddhist influence is expressed in three main categories of metalwares in central Asia: figurative representations, religious apparatus, and utensils used in both public and domestic worship. As Buddhism developed, an increasing number of symbols and motifs were added and are still commonly found on the wares of countries under Buddhist influence such as Mongolia and Tibet.

Buddhism, founded in northern India about 500 BC, spread throughout central Asia from about AD 1 to 200. Metal figures in the form of an idealised man-god were carried by missionaries and pilgrims as visual aids for prayer and meditation. Although often small, for portability, larger than life-size figures are reported in some cases. These figures are thought to have stimulated the production of representations of gods in China, where the earliest dated image of Buddha, showing strong influence from central Asia, dates from AD 338.

Buddhist figures are represented in a number of forms according to prescriptions for their proportions, postures and attributes which were laid down in India before AD 500. These forms have been elaborated and extended over time so that many differing figures reflecting local tastes are found in recent representations. Two main types of figure may be defined:

1. Images of the historic Buddha, Sakyamuni, usually depict him in monastic robes, sometimes with a halo and backed by a nimbus, sitting on a plinth or throne decorated with lotus leaves. His hair may be tightly curled over a protuberance of his skull, indicating his supernatural wisdom. One of the commonest forms of this image has the right hand stretched downwards to the earth, calling it to witness his enlightenment. These gestures or *mudras* indicate a symbolic language.

2. Bodhisattvas are beings who voluntarily delay their own liberation through compassion, until other beings are saved (figure 12). They are often shown as idealised princes and princesses wearing crowns, jewellery and flowing scarves. These figures may have several heads, arms and legs signifying various supernatural powers. They hold items of religious apparatus, including thunderbolts, a ritual chopper, skull cup, noose and magical staff. Multiple limbs indicate a later development in Buddhism.

As Buddhism developed, symbols were added to its range of expression. Metalwares such as teapots, cauldrons, food and milk containers, scabbards and pen cases are often decorated with Buddhist symbols. Most popular among these are the Eight Auspicious Symbols:

1. The lotus symbolises purity, harmony and detachment. Its eight petals remind one of the Eight Noble Truths of Buddha's teaching and may form a throne on which a Buddha or Bodhisattva rests.

2. The wheel of the law is a solar disc with eight spokes symbolising the eightfold path taught by the Buddha.

3. The vase holds all treasures and symbolises the entirety of Buddhism.

4. The conch shell is symbolic of being blessed and turning to the right path, as Buddhists do when they circumambulate sacred monuments.

5. The endless knot symbolises love, longevity and the cycle of rebirths.

6. The twin fishes symbolise happiness and freedom.

7. The royal canopy protects from the heat of desires.

8. The standard, a victory banner symbolising the attainment of enlightenment, is raised on Mount Meru, the centre of the Buddhist universe.

The lotus and the wheel have kept their religious significance, but in modern times the other six, all of pre-Buddhist Indian origin, have tended to be used as lucky symbols for decorative purposes. The endless knot, for example, is often seen on yard gates in the suburbs of Ulan Bator in the Mongolian People's Republic.

Other symbols used on Buddhist metalwares include the dragon among clouds, a sea monster, snakes, the thunderbolt, the swastika (an ancient sun symbol), and scripts including Lantsa, an archaic script based on Sanskrit, and prayers in Tibetan. On Mongolian jewellery Chinese symbols are also used, including the *shou* and double *fou* for long life and good fortune, the sceptre, the bat, the key, the dragon with a jewel (especially popular on bracelets and head-dresses), and horns, which may derive from the Animal style.

Islamic style

Islamic metalwares are primarily functional, rather than figurative or symbolic, and tend to have a few, persisting shapes. Domestic utensils include basins, ewers, dishes and vases. Lamps and incense burners are made for domestic use and in larger sizes for use in mosques.

The absence of figurative representations is one of the strongest contrasts with Buddhist artefacts. Although it was never expressly forbidden in Islam, the Arabs never had a tradition of representational art and there was a tendency to disapprove of this form of expression. However, figurative artefacts were made in most areas, albeit infrequently.

The distinctive features of Islamic metalwares are elegance of form and the complexity and variety of their surface decoration, using inlay, engraving and repoussé, techniques which have been

13. Casket of white metal decorated with scrolls in openwork; Iran; eighteenth century AD. Scroll and flower motifs, known as arabesque, are of major importance in Islamic art. 24 by 16 by 16 cm. (Horniman Museum.)

a feature of Islamic wares from the time of the adoption of Islam in central Asia to the present.

Islam was founded by Mohammed in Arabia in AD 610. The religion spread and by 740 the Islamic empire stretched from Spain to central Asia. Here the towns and cities increased their reputation for the production of fine metalwares in copper, silver, iron, pewter and especially brass or bronze.

The most typical Islamic motif is the arabesque, a plant scroll in the form of a vine, with stem, leaves and tendrils, which allows the craftsman to display an endless variation of surface decoration and symbolises the infinity of Allah (figure 13). Several influences affected the development of this style, including earlier Iranian motifs, derived in part from central Asia, such as stylised repetitive patterns of palmettes and rosettes, and fantastic creatures including griffins, winged lions, and humans with animal heads. Incense burners are made in animal, bird or human form, and ewers with long spouts and handles reflect Greek influence. Arabic inscriptions in various scripts including angular Kufic and cursive Nakshi were added to these items.

Recent Islamic wares still show the influences of early Islam, India, the Mediterranean and east Asia. Today in the Muslim republics of Soviet Central Asia the hammer and sickle, peace emblems, including doves, and the Kremlin have been added to the traditional motifs used on Islamic metalwares.

14. Detail of the base of a tea bowl decorated with copper scrollwork showing the deep undercutting technique which is characteristic of Mongolian metalworking; Mongolian People's Republic; modern. (Horniman Museum.)

Decorative techniques

A wide range of decorative techniques are used on central Asian metalwares. Some techniques are practised throughout the region, others are particular to a place or area.

Appliqué: decorated metal plaques are soldered on to the surface of the artefact. This is a feature of Buddhist metalwares, teapots and food containers for example, as well as Yomut Turkmen jewellery.

Chasing: patterns are punched into the surface with a hammer and a tracer chisel. No metal is removed in this technique, which may leave uneven marks if the craftsman is unskilled. The Uzbeks and Tadzhiks are renowned for their chased copperwares.

Engraving: a design is cut into the surface with a chisel or graver, which removes a sliver of metal. This technique is used throughout central Asia. In Mongolia a technique of deep undercutting is practised (figure 14).

Filigree: thin wire, produced by drawing it through smaller and smaller holes in a drawing plate, is soldered on to a backing metal to form patterns (figure 15). Khiva was noted for its filigree work, although this technique was more common in eastern central Asia. The Tibetans were renowned for filigree, which is also a feature of Mongolian jewellery.

Fire gilding: gold dust is mixed with mercury and the mixture is applied to the metal artefact, which is then heated; the mercury evaporates and the gold is fused to the metal surface. It is finished by polishing. This technique is used on Turkmen jewellery.

Gallery wire: wire is wound around nails on a board, then removed and soldered to the backing metal. This technique was commonly used on jewellery in west central Asia (figure 16).

Gilding: a thin layer of gold leaf is laid or painted on the surface of a metal object. Tibetan figures were often finished in this way.

Granulation: many tiny metal globules are soldered to a backing metal. This technique is used in Uzbek jewellery and in Tibetan wares such as amulet cases.

Inlay: various materials are inlaid into the surface of metal artefacts:
Enamel. Molten coloured glass is fused on to the surface of the object, either into channels cut in the surface (*champlevé*) or into cells (*cloisonné*) formed by soldering thin metal strips on to the surface. Bukhara was noted for its enamel work. It is also a

15. (Left and below) Pendant and detail to show filigree work; Kazakh, Kazakhstan, USSR; about 1900 AD. Filigree is produced by soldering fine wires on to sheet metal. (Museum of Mankind.)

16. Necklace made from interlocking pieces of white metal decorated with twisted wire in spiral motifs on box fitting made from strips of sheet metal; Iran; 15 cm. (Horniman Museum.)

feature of some Mongolian jewellery and may have been brought eastwards from Asia Minor during the period of the Mongol empire.

Niello. An alloy of silver, lead and copper is smelted into channels and hollows cut into a metal surface, then finished by smoothing and polishing. Bukhara was famous for this technique.

Precious stones might also be inlaid, such as turquoise and coral in Tibetan and Mongolian wares, carnelians in Turkmen jewellery. Box settings are commonly used in Turkmen jewellery: strips of sheet metal soldered to the base plate are pressed over the stone along their upper edges to hold it in place.

Wax, mastic and *glass* were also inlaid on metal objects. Bukhara produced objects inlaid with mirror glass, and red, blue and green mastics were used to fill the backgrounds of decorations on brass vessels. The use of these materials indicates influences from Kashmir and northern India. Black and red lacquer inlay on a punched background was also a feature of west central Asian wares at the end of the nineteenth century.

Damascening. Inlays of gold, silver or copper are hammered into grooves cut in the surface of an iron, steel or bronze object (figure 17). This technique, a particular feature of Islamic wares, including utensils, lamps, weapons and horse harness, is also used on some wares from Derge in eastern Tibet, such as beer jugs, soup jars, water bottles and figures.

Openwork or **piercing:** the metal is carved away with a hammer and chisel to give an effect of tracery. This technique shows Iranian influence and is used for decorative effect on a variety of wares including boxes, incense burners, jewellery and weapons (figure 18).

Overlay: sheet metal is hammered on to a prepared metal surface. Two methods are used: thin sheets of gold or silver foil are hammered on to the background metal, usually iron or steel, and are secured by grooves cut around the outlines of the design; or the ground metal is scored or cross-hatched with fine lines cut with a chisel, then the gold or silver sheet is hammered on. This technique, also called *koftgari*, became popular from the fifteenth century onwards and was especially used as decoration on weapons.

Repoussé: relief patterns are punched into the metal sheet from the inside, against a soft anvil such as a block of pitch or a sandbag. The relief may then be outlined by chasing around it from the outside.

17. Wooden casket covered with iron sheet inlaid with silver; Kazakh, Kazakhstan; about 1900; 8.1 by 5 by 5 cm. (Museum of Mankind.)

18. Detail of a peacock with a brass openwork body and glass insets for the eyes; Iran; nineteenth century AD; height 50 cm. In western central Asia openwork is produced by cutting through the sheet metal with hammer and chisel. (Horniman Museum.)

Stamping: punches with patterned surfaces are hammered on the surface to form patterns.

Welding and forging: a variety of effects is obtained by forging or hammering iron and steel whilst hot.

Watered steel is produced from iron which is mixed with wood and charcoal in a clay-sealed crucible, heated for a long time and then allowed to cool slowly. This process produces high-carbon steel (wootz), in which the crystals have been rearranged. When the ingot is forged into a sword-blade or other weapon, a pattern of wavy lines appears on the surface. This pattern may be emphasised by etching the surface with acid, which reacts differently to the different crystals, producing a 'watered' or damask effect. This process was especially popular as decoration for Islamic weapons, armour, firearms and some utensils.

Pattern welding is also used for decoration: iron and steel ingots are repeatedly twisted and folded together during forging. When the finished product is polished, light and dark bands appear according to the hardness of the metals. If the surface is then etched with acid, the softer iron is eaten away and the pattern stands out even more.

A pattern known as the *Forty Steps* or *Mohammed's Ladder* was produced in some Islamic sword-blades, including those from Khorasan, by cutting grooves across the width of a blade before completing the forging.

4
Forms and functions

Tools and utensils

Metalwares relating to economic life in central Asia include utensils, tools and implements used in the domestic economy, and products for trade and the tourist market.

Agricultural implements include the scratch plough with an iron share, either ox-drawn or horse-drawn, which is used in oases and settled communities and by sedentary nomads. In Tuva a heavier plough with a cast iron mouldboard for turning the soil was used. Oasis fields are irrigated from canals or dammed streams, and there is additional cultivation on drier uplands. Hoes, spades, picks and mattocks are generally used. Harvesting tools include scythes and sickles. In Mongolia, where agriculture tended to be a despised occupation, a long-handled sickle was developed to cut grass, to avoid the stooping entailed in the use of the short-handled Chinese sickle. Pick-like hoes are used by the Tibetans for harvesting root crops. Axes and adzes are used for cutting and working wood.

Agricultural implements from central Asia are uncommon in museum collections, but eating and cooking utensils made from iron and steel may be seen. These include trivets, vegetable cutters and scrapers, knives, spoons (figure 19), ladles, flint and steel and miscellaneous ferrous wares (for example the melon knife, figure 20). Melons are a major crop in the sandy regions of central Asia. Locks were formerly ornate and decorative objects (figure 21), but now they are often factory-made imports. Steel surgical implements were used in traditional medicine.

Iron and copper cooking pots and pans were both imported and made locally. The Kazakhs traditionally cooked in a cauldron suspended from an iron tripod. In Mongolia a high cylindrical iron trivet was used. Cast iron cooking pots with a rounded base and lug-shaped handles on the rim are of Russian manufacture and are imported to both western central Asia and Mongolia. A circular iron sheet is used for baking flat bread, which is basic to the diet of Muslim central Asia.

A set of kitchen utensils was an essential part of a bride's dowry in Islamic society; it would have included water jugs, basins and ewers, dishes, trays, vases, lamps, stoves and incense burners.

One of the distinctive types of central Asian metalwares is the ewer, a tall jug with a long spout and a loop handle. This shape, which may derive from an Iranian form, is used in Islamic central Asia for the ablutions which are essential before saying prayers. The ewer is also used in Buddhist central Asia for ritual offerings of water to the gods, both at home and in the temples (figure 22). Tibetan and Mongolian ewers are often decorated with Buddhist symbols including lotus leaves and a monster's head around the spout. Islamic bowls and dishes for serving liquids such as sherbet and wine occur in both pedestal and round-based forms.

Metal food containers and pails for storing milk, water and beer are part of nomadic equipment (figure 23). These are usually cylindrical with a low domed lid. In Tibet and Mongolia they are often decorated with metal strapping and appliqué. Fine beer jugs and water flasks of damascened iron, used when camping or travelling, are a feature of eastern Tibetan wares. Trade and the extensive travelling it entailed were an integral part of Tibetan life for settled people and nomads, monks and laymen.

19. (Right) Spoon for pilau, with a white metal bowl in openwork; Bukhara, Uzbek SSR; nineteenth century AD; 39 by 12 cm. (Horniman Museum.)

20. (Below) Steel melon knife; Aksu, Xinjiang, China; length 19.5 cm. (Horniman Museum.)

Lighting in mosques was traditionally by means of oil lamps either in vase form or in glass contained in openwork metal cases suspended from the ceiling by chains. Bukhara was famous for its production of copper lamps. Candlesticks shaped like a heavy cylinder, with inward curving sides on which the candle socket is fixed, were also commonly used. In Buddhist countries lighting was usually by means of butter lamps. A cylindrical bowl with outward sloping sides on a pedestal with a flared base holds a wick floating in melted butter or mustard oil. Lamps such as these are found especially in a religious context, either on the domestic altar or in temples, where numerous lamps are lit on special occasions and to honour important deities.

Tea drinking plays an important part in central Asian society. In western central Asia the samovar, a Russian invention, was generally adopted during the nineteenth century. In Buddhist central Asia considerable quantities of tea were drunk in homes and in monasteries. Tibetan teapots are made in a variety of

21. Locks and keys of inlaid iron. (Right) Tibet. (Below) Khotan, Xinjiang, China. (Horniman Museum.)

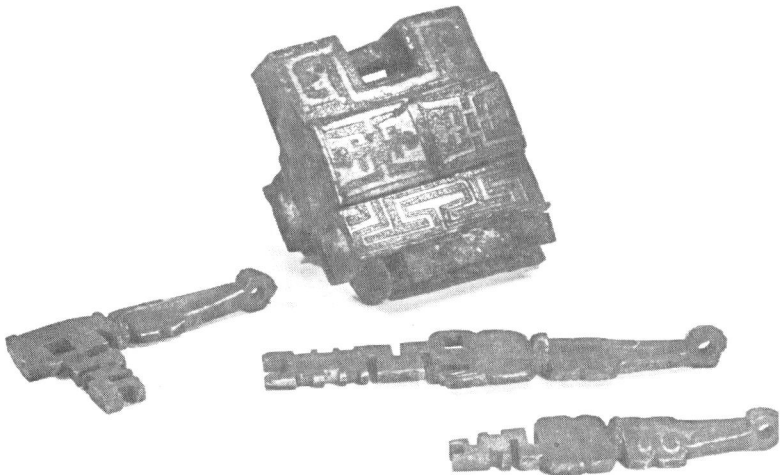

22. Ewer of copper and white metal decorated with appliqué panels on the sides of the body. Used for libations, this is an example of modern Tibetan work. Height 26 cm.

forms from globular to a truncated cone shape with angular shoulders. Metal teapots, often highly decorated with gold and silver bands on copper and with applied Buddhist symbols, were used for ceremonies and festivals including New Year and marriages. Earthenware and wooden teapots, from which the tea tastes better, were used for everyday purposes. Tibetan teapots reflect a mixture of influences in their form, including Iranian and Chinese, whilst western central Asian teapots tend to be decorated with the engraving and stamping typical of Islamic metalwares.

In Tibetan ceremonies, where tea was drunk in quantity by numerous monks, it was brewed in cauldrons made of copper and other alloys, including bell-metal (figure 25). Large copper cauldrons decorated with brass appliqué are exported from Nepal to Tibet today.

23. (Above) Two copper and brass food containers. (Left) Decorated with chased scrolls and appliqué panels and straps, with a bossed lid and rings for carrying straps; Tibet; twentieth century AD; height 30 cm. (Right) A body of plain copper sheet decorated with appliqué brass plaques engraved with scrolls; Mongolian People's Republic; modern; height 32 cm. (Horniman Museum.)

24. (Right) Domestic tea jug made of brass; Mongolian People's Republic; early twentieth century AD; height 44 cm. (Horniman Museum.)

25. Copper tea cauldrons; Lhasa, Tibet; 1920s. Cauldrons such as these are used to make tea for large numbers of monks during religious ceremonies. (Pitt Rivers Museum.)

Religious figures and apparatus

Central Asian religious metalwares consist primarily of Buddhist figurative items and apparatus. Some of these artefacts were used for domestic and public worship. Tibetan and Mongolian wares show such close similarities that it is not always possible to differentiate them.

Buddhist religious figures, made in a variety of metals, are used as aids to meditation and prayer. Religious apparatus includes sets of offering bowls, butter lamps, vases, incense burners, musical instruments, notably long telescopic copper trumpets and cymbals, and some metal masks. Offerings of water, food, flowers and incense are made daily.

Implements used by lamas in particular rituals include a bell, symbolising wisdom, and a ritual thunderbolt symbolising religious method. A triangular-bladed dagger, often made from bronze, is used to control evil spirits.

Prayer-wheels are a particular feature of Tibetan culture. They consist of a cylinder, usually copper or bronze, rotating around a central iron spindle and containing prayers written on rolls of

26. Buddhist religious apparatus; Tibet; early twentieth century AD. (From top left to bottom right) A bell, symbolising wisdom; a mirror, symbol of visible things; a libation vessel, to make the offering of water; and a butter lamp, to make the offering of light. (Horniman Museum.)

27. Prayer-wheels with Lantsa script, Gandan Temple, Ulan Bator, Mongolian People's Republic.

paper. The wheel may be rotated by hand or, in different forms, by running water, the wind or hot air from a lamp or candle. The Tibetans believe that spiritual merit is gained by the repetition of prayers in this way. Prayer-wheels are often decorated with Buddhist figures, symbols and letters in an archaic script called Lantsa (figure 27). Amulet cases, often ornate, containing small images of the gods and prayers written on paper, are worn in the Buddhist countries (figure 28).

Jewellery

Precious metals are highly regarded throughout central Asia, and jewellery serves as an indication of social rank, as portable wealth and as a protection against accidents and malign influences. Knives and horse harness (bridle, bit, straps and saddles) decorated with gold and silver inlay also indicate status (figures 29 and 30).

Wealthy town dwellers traditionally used a number of metal accessories including decorated belt buckles, toilet implements with earspoons, picks and tweezers, and flint and steel. Wealthy nomads in Mongolia would also have silver-mounted tea bowls, snuff bottles and amulet cases. Poorer people, both urban and nomadic, wore much less jewellery, often consisting of imitation stones and base metals.

28. Three amulet cases of copper and brass; Tibet; each 9.2 by 8 cm. One amulet case of brass with turquoise insets (top right); Tibet; 6 by 6 cm. (Horniman Museum.)

29. Horse harness: bridle, girth, crupper and whip; steel with silver mounts and carnelian insets; Turkmen, Iran; early twentieth century AD. (Whitworth Art Gallery.)

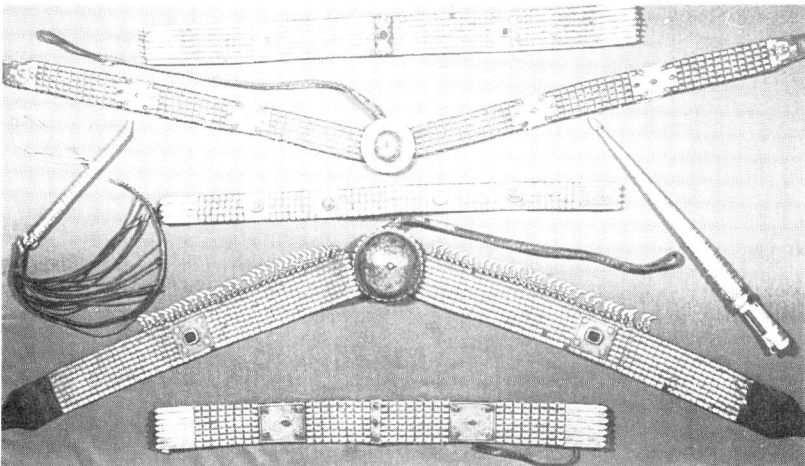

30. (Left) Saddle with silver mounts and iron stirrups; Mongolian People's Republic; modern. (Horniman Museum.)

31. (Right) A man's belongings; western Mongolia; modern. A root-wood tea bowl with silver lining and pedestal, a pipe with a machine-made steel bowl, two tobacco pouches with silver clasps and a silver pipe cleaner. (Copyright: K. Chabros.)

Gold and silver jewellery was set with semi-precious stones, including carnelians, popular among the Turkmen, and turquoise. Saddle-cloths embroidered with gold and silver thread are popular in the cities of western central Asia.

Men's jewellery generally consisted of useful items such as the knives and toilet implements already noted, while women wore purely ornamental pieces. Both sexes wear finger rings. Today women tend to preserve their cultural identity in their use of jewellery and dress, but men have largely adopted Western dress and abandoned wearing jewellery and ornate swords and daggers.

There are differences in the jewellery of various tribal and national groupings, although these are often shaded rather than sharply defined. A tendency to amalgamate pieces makes provenancing difficult in some cases. Jewellers in towns and oases made most of the jewellery for both town dwellers and nomads. That for the nomads was often made to order, in more elaborate and varied styles than for urban customers.

Nomadic jewellery from before the mid nineteenth century is difficult to date. In western central Asia it shows influences from Animal style in the use of motifs such as the trefoil, wave, hook, fork leaf runner and double-headed eagle. Islamic motifs are also used, including the arabesque, symbol of Allah's infinity, and floral shapes. Earlier pieces are made of finer materials with clearer shapes and decoration, larger carnelians and fewer glass beads.

The Turkmen tribes living along the borders of the Soviet Union, Iran and northern Afghanistan are renowned for their jewellery. Silver is preferred, with insets of carnelian, the most popular stone, which is thought to bring peace to the individual and friendship between people. Turquoise is also used. In the nineteenth century coins from Russia, Iran and China were melted down for their silver, since local silver was no longer mined. Pearls, coral and glass beads were imported from India and Europe.

Different tribes of Turkmen prefer different forms and decorative techniques. Teke jewellery consists of heavy pieces

32. Turkmen girls in their holiday finery, wearing skullcaps and pendant head-dress ornaments, *chekelik*. The silver finials, *gupba*, of their skullcaps show that the girls are unmarried. Turkmenia, Soviet Central Asia. (Photograph: J. Thompson.)

with a fire-gilded ground inset with carnelians and glass beads (figure 33), whilst the Ersari prefer lighter pieces of pure silver, with no fire gilding, fewer carnelians and no gallery wire. Saryk jewellery, by contrast, makes great use of gallery wire. Among the Yomut, some groups favour fire gilding, whilst others do not.

The glory and variety of Turkmen jewellery is best seen in the adornments worn by the nomadic herdswomen. There is a wide variety of these, including head pieces, bridal crowns, caps, hair pieces and pendants, necklaces and pectoral decorations, earrings, collar studs, bracelets, belts and finger rings. Turkmen women used to wear large amounts of jewellery whilst working and sleeping: 6 to 8 kg in weight was commonplace, and 17 kg of bridal jewellery has been reported. Today they tend to reserve their jewellery for wearing at festivals and ceremonies.

Jewellery is also used in central Asia as a protection against misfortune. Among the Turkmen the face is thought to be vulnerable, hence the use of silver, turquoise and blue beads to ward off the evil eye, and of bloodstone against bleeding. Children wear silver talismans as protection; boys may wear a brooch shaped like a bow and arrow for this purpose. Turkmen women's jewellery was more elaborate than that of oasis women and other nomadic tribes such as the Kazakh and Kirghiz.

Wealthier Kazakhs traditionally acquired jewellery from itinerant silversmiths who made various items to order: hair ornaments, pendants, earrings, bracelets, rings, belt buckles and decorative horse harness in iron or wood with silver inlay. Kazakh jewellery is also inset with carnelians and other semi-precious stones similar to some Turkmen jewellery; some gold filigree work also occurs. Decoration consists of incised, often stylised geometric motifs: lines, triangles, diamonds, circles and spirals.

The craftsmanship of urban jewellers in western central Asia declined in the late nineteenth century. Much thinner silver sheet was used with stamped decoration and putty filling. European objects, for example tiepins with turquoise inlay, began to be made for the Russian market. Today silverworking is almost extinct among the Kazakh and Kirghiz and is declining among the Turkmen.

Traditional jewellery is also no longer worn daily in eastern central Asia. Mongolian married women used to wear head-dresses whose shape and materials indicated their tribal group. The Khalkha of Outer Mongolia wore large head-dresses in gold and silver formed like down-sloping cows' horns. A silver or gilt

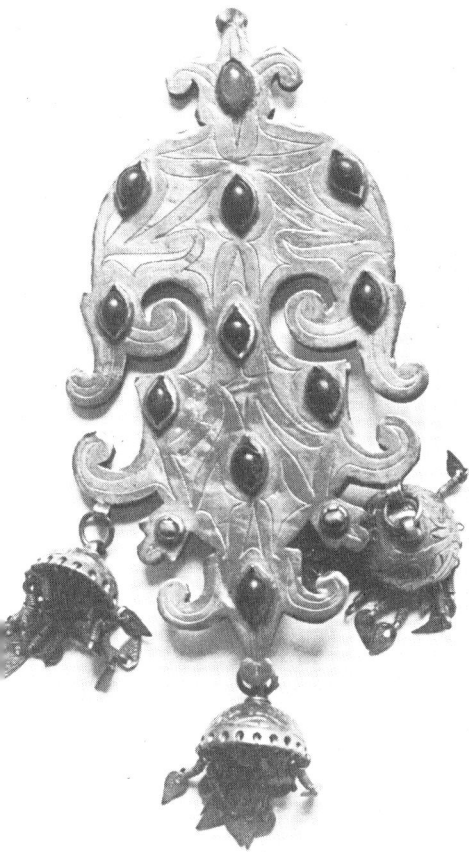

33. (Left) Breast ornament; Turkmen, Iran; 18 by 10 cm. Fire-gilded silver incised with dotted lines, with insets of carnelians and turquoise; with three pendant domes, each with leaf-shaped pendants suspended on twisted wire and decorated with incised scrolls. (Horniman Museum.)

34. (Above) Pair of earrings in white metal; Tashkent, Uzbek SSR; length 25 cm. (Museum of Mankind.)

skullcap with three pendants, perhaps inlaid with pearls, was worn by unmarried girls. Outer Mongolians always valued silver for its purity, whilst Inner Mongolians preferred coral and precious stones, with silver as a secondary material. Silver was used for men's possessions such as saddles, knives and eating sets, belt rings, tea bowls and snuff bottles. All these might have silver mounts and were decorated according to the wealth and social status of the owner.

Earrings or pendants with an ear hook for attachment were formerly worn, along with bracelets and finger rings of chased or filigreed silver inset with coral, amber and precious stones such as turquoise, rubies, emeralds and pearls. Silver coinage was popular for jewellery.

Precise provenancing is not possible in this region, since sets of jewellery were split and recombined. Chinese craftsmen combined Mongolian and Chinese elements to cater for local tastes among the aristocracy. Noble Chinese women were frequently married to Mongol lords in order to secure their allegiance to the Chinese. Smiths also tended to blur tribal

Metalcrafts of Central Asia

differences in their products. During the Qing or Manchu period of domination in Mongolia (1644-1912) jewellery reached the peak of development as the Mongols became increasingly dependent on the Chinese for silver and other materials.

Some of the earliest records, from the T'ang period in China (AD 618-906), refer to the skill of the Tibetans in working precious metals. The Tibetans also used a variety of other materials in their jewellery: coral, turquoise, pearls, emeralds, lapis lazuli, rock crystal, jade and amber. Precious stones were also inset into religious figures and utensils. In the nineteenth century such materials were often replaced by poor-quality coloured glass. Tibetan 'amber' for example may contain imitation material made from a mixture of powdered amber, copal and artificial colouring.

Various beliefs are associated with different materials in Buddhist central Asia. Turquoise, often inset into amulets or charm boxes, was thought to strengthen bones against the effects of falling off a horse, and, when swallowed, it was thought to cure poisoning. Jade, worn by the wealthy, was also thought to strengthen the bones. An ivory ring, worn by a man on his left thumb, was protection against witches. Both men and women wore gold or silver finger rings, often containing charms (figure 35).

Jewellery also indicated social status. A man's long earring and gold and turquoise hair brooch indicated official rank. Unmarried

35. Finger rings of silver with turquoise and glass insets; Tibet; about 1900. (Horniman Museum.)

36. (Left) Ear ornaments of silver, turquoise and wool; Tibet; early twentieth century AD. (Horniman Museum.)

37. (Below) Breast ornament made from engraved sheet brass; western Tibet; 15 by 9 cm. (Horniman Museum.)

38. (Above) Nomad woman with a headdress of beaten silver discs. Golok, Sino-Tibetan border. (Pitt Rivers Museum.)

girls wore coral on top of their head-dress, whilst married women wore a turquoise over coral on theirs; the removal of these ornaments indicated legal separation. Women wore a variety of jewelled head-dresses as well as pendant earrings and plain pendants inlaid with turquoise, hairclips, and coins or coral set in gold and silver mounts. Nomad women wore felt head-dresses decorated with silver, coral and turquoise plates or medallions as well as coins (figure 38).

Weapons and armour
    The main weapons used by central Asian peoples were swords, axes, maces, daggers, bows, lances and, in modern times, firearms. Axes originated in pre-Islamic times and rivalled the sword in importance. In the Hindu Kush and the Karakorum axes are still used on ceremonial occasions in ritual dances. They also form part of bridewealth. Axes (figure 39) and maces were carried as symbols of office and as weapons by generals and leaders in medieval and modern times, amongst both Muslims and Mongols.
    Two main sword types occur up to modern times: a curved scimitar (*shamshir* in Persian), and a long straight-bladed sword as used in Tibet (figure 40). It is not known when the curved sword was introduced. Frescoes dating from the ninth century AD in Turkestan show curved, single-edged swords in use. The

39. Battleaxe; Bukhara, Uzbek SSR; nineteenth century AD; blade 14.5 by 11 cm. The steel blade has engraved decoration; the haft is of painted wood. The battleaxe has rivalled the sword in western central Asian arms. (Horniman Museum.)

40. (Left) Sword and sheath decorated with chased metal mounts; eastern Tibet; twentieth century AD. Swords such as this have continued in use until the present. (Horniman Museum.)

41. (Right) Copper helmet decorated with archaic Lantsa script; Tibet; nineteenth century AD. (Horniman Museum.)

use of curved swords spread during the Mongol invasions in the thirteenth century, although they may have used a straight sword originally. The scimitar has a regularly curved, single-edged blade with a cross-guard. The Iranian form has a tapering tip, whilst the Turkish form has a broad tip and an angular curve. The Indian *tulwar*, although derived from the Iranian form, has a broader blade and is less curved than the *shamshir*. In the sixteenth century Iranian swords developed a grip with short quillons and round knobs and with a pommel cap set at right angles to the main part of the grip.

Dating swords is difficult: blades might be reused and imported from elsewhere, and Iranian blades were exported throughout the Islamic world. Later blades tend to be shorter and narrower. Some have the owner's name inlaid in gold. The finest blades were etched to produce a 'watered' effect (see chapter 3). Many of the finest swords were made in Khorasan, in north-eastern Iran, and Kokand in the mid nineteenth century. Local peoples such as the Turkmen were armed with Iranian blades produced by urban swordmakers until the Russian conquest. Until the late nineteenth century the Turkmen also used a lance consisting of an iron tip on a cane shaft.

In eastern central Asia the Khambas used swords with some effect against the Chinese in 1950. In Tibet a straight-bladed, single-edged sword was commonly used. This has a small disc guard and a blunt point. The blade might be imported from China, India or Bhutan, which was said to provide the best swords for central Tibet, whilst the metalworkers of Derge had the highest reputation in eastern Tibet. Decoration often comprises silver mounts on the hilt and scabbard. Daggers, often highly decorated with inlay and engraving or with silver wirework and mounts, were also an essential part of a man's dress until recently.

The earliest Chinese sources about Tibet refer to Tibetan skill in working iron for armour. Armour is thought to have been introduced to Tibet from the eastern region of Kham. During the seventh and eighth centuries AD the Tibetans had an extensive empire in central Asia, won by their military prowess. Recent Tibetan armour is made of iron scales on thongs overlapping upwards, whilst Islamic armour is a composite of chain-mail and plate used for chest and arm guards. Forms of armour are less varied and changing than in western Europe.

From the sixteenth and seventeenth centuries onwards firearms were gradually adopted throughout central Asia. Matchlocks, probably traded from India, were introduced to Iran and western central Asia. Iranian gunsmiths then started to produce watered steel barrels, often decorated with engraved chevron motifs and inlaid with calligraphy giving the owners' and makers' names. Iranian firearms were traded on a wide scale in Asia. Western central Asian firearms have the barrel attached with brass bands and have a down-curving 'jezail' stock.

Tibetan and Mongolian muskets are of cruder manufacture, made from iron parts imported from China mounted on a straight wooden stock which may have a covering of skin sewn on. A characteristic feature is a two-pronged fork-rest of wood, sometimes with horn or iron tips, which is pivoted on the lower side of the stock. These muskets vary in length from 0.9 to 1.5 metres and some are decorated with an inlay of silver, brass or bone.

Modern firearms became widely available in western central Asia from about 1860 onwards. The first native gunsmiths in Turkestan started working only in the 1880s. However, the skill of modern Afghan gunsmiths in copying modern firearms in workshops with only the most basic equipment is well known.

5
Metals and their manufacture

Central Asia is especially rich in minerals: copper, tin, gold, silver and iron are all found throughout the region; zinc and lead occur in western areas and in the Altai, a particularly rich source of most metals, where extensive mining has been carried on since the early eighteenth century. Similar large-scale mining has occurred in Xinjiang in the nineteenth and early twentieth centuries.

During the twentieth century, following the establishment of communist regimes in the USSR and Mongolia, major prospecting and mining has been undertaken to develop metal deposits. Massive deposits of coal and a variety of metal ores, including one of the largest deposits of copper in the world, were discovered in Kazakhstan. This mining region, around Lake Balkhash, and the region further south in Uzbekistan and Fergana are now of primary importance in the Soviet economy. Tibet, potentially one of the richest metal-bearing areas in the world, was relatively undeveloped during the first half of the twentieth century, although mining did occur along the Sino-Tibetan border.

Metals, especially gold and silver, have been imported into central Asia from ancient times: from Europe via the Mediterranean; from Japan; from Mexico and Peru; and from Russia and India, especially during the nineteenth century. As the Western nations and Russia became industrialised, sheet metal (copper, brass and iron) has been supplied to central Asian markets either as finished goods or as raw material to be refashioned for local consumption or export.

Metals occur in two forms, either in relatively pure or 'native' form, usually in small amounts, or more often as ores, where the metal is in combination with other materials such as rocks or clay. Metal-bearing ores are distributed irregularly throughout the world. Iron ores are particularly common, whilst other metals, gold and silver for example, are rarer. Ore deposits occur both on the surface and at deeper levels in the earth. After extraction ores are treated by fire (smelting) to produce workable metals.

Extraction

Copper was the first metal to be exploited in the highland zones surrounding what is now Iraq, from about 8000 to 4000 BC.

North-eastern Iran was one of the regions which supplied copper for the tools and ornaments of Mesopotamian societies. By 4000 BC copper implements were in use in western central Asia.

Copper is obtained from two main groups of ores: oxidised ores, including cuprite, azurite and malachite; and sulphide ores, including copper pyrites and chalcocite.

The bright green-blue colour of some oxidised ores such as malachite makes them easily noticeable when they occur as surface deposits, and it was probably these ores which were first worked in quantity. Surface ores can be collected by 'grubbing' from open-cast workings with picks, or they may be split from rocks by setting fires against them and then quenching the heated rock with water.

Sulphide ores occur underground and deep-mining techniques using shafts and galleries are needed to extract them. The ores are hacked from the rock with hammers, picks, wedges and levers. Deep mining was established in the Near East by about 3000 BC as copper extraction increased in scale. In 1908 a Russian expedition visited a copper mine 11 metres deep, which was at least two thousand years old, near Kokand in Fergana. Descent into deep mines was either by ladders or in a bucket on a rope, which was also the means by which the excavated ore was raised.

If copper is alloyed or mixed with other suitable metals it becomes easier to work and stronger objects may be produced. An alloy of tin and copper produces bronze, which was first developed about 3500 BC in the Iraq/Iran area and then spread to central Asia. Tin deposits are relatively rare and this metal was carried for long distances in ancient times: the route from Cornwall to the eastern Mediterranean is a well known example. In central Asia tin deposits occur in Kazakhstan, the Altai, Mongolia and the Mongolian-Siberian border. Tinstone (cassiterite) often occurs in the same deposits as alluvial gold and was perhaps discovered and extracted in the same way originally — by washing or panning from stream deposits.

Brass, an alloy of copper and zinc, was invented in the Roman period, later than bronze. At first brass was difficult to produce because zinc tended to vaporise during extraction from its ore, calamine. Zinc is often found with lead deposits, which are extensive in western central Asia and the Altai.

In prehistoric times copper was probably extracted from ores with over 15 per cent metal content, and in the middle ages from ores with about 8 per cent metal content. Today copper is extracted from ores with 0.65 per cent metal content. It is only since the late nineteenth century that developments in mining and extraction techniques have enabled ores with such a low metallic content to be exploited.

Iron or ferrous ores are much more widespread than non-ferrous deposits and are found in a variety of 'ironstones', including haematite and limonite, recognisable by their weight and texture. These ores can be acquired by grubbing the surface of the earth with simple tools such as digging sticks and picks. Numerous small deposits provide for the local manufacture of iron objects. Deep mines are sunk where extensive deposits occur.

Large iron ore deposits occur throughout central Asia, with especially rich ones in Kazakhstan, the Altai and around Derge in eastern Tibet. Deposits in China and Russia, especially the Urals, have long been sources of iron for central Asia.

Metalware production

Ironworking developed from about 2000 BC in western Asia and spread slowly over the next thousand years. It was practised on the western steppes by about 900 BC, when the first mounted nomadic societies are recorded there. These peoples, known as the Scyths or Scythians, were formed into kingdoms whose courts used weapons and armour made by blacksmiths and the decorative and ornamental products of goldsmiths. As with bronze working, the nomadic peoples of central Asia probably contributed to the subsequent rapid spread of ironworking to China.

Objects made from iron, primarily weapons, armour and tools, were made for local consumption and for export. In the middle ages Fergana and Khorasan were famous for the arms and armour which they exported throughout the Muslim world.

Before the nineteenth century metalware production of both non-ferrous and ferrous wares was based on abundant local ores. The increasing influence of the surrounding powers, notably Russia, China and the British in India, led to dependence on imports. Central Asian craftworking, especially in metal, was affected by the impact of the products of industrialisation. Local deposits of ores were no longer worked. Sheet copper, brass and iron were imported along with factory-made goods. The cities of central Asia now made their wares from imported raw materials or distributed manufactured metalwares imported from India and Russia throughout the region. Around 1900 the Singer Sewing Machine Company had an enormous warehouse in Kazakhstan, which served as the site of a fair and a centre for the distribution of imported goods throughout central Asia as far as Siberia. A sewing machine is still a high-status possession amongst nomadic peoples.

During the nineteenth century blacksmiths in rural areas were reduced to tinkering and small-scale manufacturing. Their source of metal was old iron vessels and tools, which they melted down and recast or worked into new products. They also used ingots which they or their customers bought from traders and merchants. Many rural smiths today rely heavily on scrap metal, lorry springs and railway line, the products of industry, for their raw material.

From the 1920s the Russians started to work major iron deposits in Kazakhstan, the Altai and western Siberia. Mining also began to be developed in Xinjiang and the Mongolian People's Republic.

Precious metals

Although rarer than base metals, gold deposits are relatively widespread in central Asia, especially in the Pamirs, the Altai and Tibet, which is reckoned to be potentially the richest gold-producing land in the world. Gold came into use about 4000 BC in Iraq. It is found as deposits of dust and grains in streams and river beds, washed down from deposits in higher ground, or as nuggets and seams in quartz rocks.

Gold was first extracted by panning. Water and gravel are scooped up from a stream bed in a shallow dish which is swirled around to discard the water and reveal the gold by its colour. In 1921 850 kg of gold were extracted by panning at the Tacheng mines in Xinjiang, which employed ten thousand men.

Silver is generally less common than gold. It too is found as dust or grains in streams, and also as ores in combination with other metals such as lead. In central Asia deposits are found in the Altai, Mongolia, south-eastern Tibet and northern Afghanistan.

Gold and silver are also extracted by grubbing surface deposits and by deep mining. By the middle ages mines were kept clear of water by hydraulic wheels and the ore-bearing clay was brought to the surface for extraction. Although this operation required a heavy investment of capital and was labour-intensive, it could give high yields. Around Herat, crude ore mined in this way yielded one-quarter of its weight in pure silver. Mines were

42. Coin necklace or breast ornament; Afghanistan; 1920s; 27 by 20 cm. Gold and silver coins on a horseshoe-shaped base, decorated with incised dots and bands in cross-hatching and diagonals or chevrons; inset with blue turquoise on the central panels, which also have gold and silver filigree and granulations. The coins are a mixture of Afghan and Iranian coins with script, animal and human motifs, and Indian annas dating from the nineteenth and early twentieth centuries, the newest dated 1910. (Horniman Museum.)

abandoned when deposits and local fuel supplies for smelting were exhausted, or when they became too deep to work.

Trade in metals

Artefacts made of metal, especially precious metals, can be melted down and reshaped according to fashion or other circumstances, and metal coins may be used for decorative purposes rather than currency.

Gold and silver entered central Asia from a variety of sources in the form of bullion and coinage. The Romans paid in this way for Chinese silks and spices traded along the Silk Route. The Chinese have traded with the nomads of central Asia for gold from the Altai and Tibet for over two thousand years. From AD *c.*700 gold and silver from Japan were also exported into China, which tempted the Mongols to invade Japan in the thirteenth century. The Arabs probably exported East African gold into central Asia and in the middle ages the flow of European gold and silver into this region continued along the overland trade routes.

After the Americas were discovered by Europeans in 1492, the flow of precious metals into central and eastern Asia increased. Sea traffic developed from America via the Philippines to China. This 'Manila trade' lasted from 1573 to 1815. Chinese and central Asian demand was enormous well into the twentieth century. Coinage such as Mexican dollars, Peruvian pesos, Maria Theresa dollars, Russian roubles and Indian annas was used as ornaments and jewellery by the nomadic peoples, notably the Turkmen, Kirghiz and Mongolians (figure 42). Coins were also melted down to serve as raw material for jewellery. Conversely lumps of unworked precious metals and turquoise served as currency in eastern central Asia about 1900.

Precious materials such as turquoise from eastern Iran, Fergana and Kazakhstan, lapis lazuli from northern Afghanistan, diamonds and carnelians from India and pearls, amber and coral from the Mediterranean have been popular in central Asia for centuries.

Non-ferrous metalworking

After extraction, ores must be washed to remove earthy materials and then refined, or smelted in a furnace, to obtain usable metal.

Copper oxide ores are reduced to copper by direct smelting: the ore is mixed with charcoal and heated in a simple furnace. A bowl furnace consists of a clay-lined bowl in the ground with a clay blow-tube, or tuyère, leading into it. This air hole may be angled towards the wind, but more commonly a bellows, a bag of skin or leather, is attached to the blow-tube to give the draught which is essential to heat the ore and fuel. The smelt of liquefied metal flows to the bottom of the furnace whilst less dense waste material, the slag, floats on top and can be removed.

Sulphide ores contain more clay and gravel material, including silica and limestone. These materials have to be removed by hammering and washing away. The ore is then dried and roasted to remove the sulphur ready for smelting. The presence of sulphur in metals makes them brittle, resulting in areas of weakness. If copper sulphide ores have not been reduced by frequent raking during the roasting process, the resulting copper is full of blow-holes, known as 'blister copper'. This requires a second smelting to refine it. Roasting also makes metal more friable and easier to work.

Bowl furnaces are inadequate for large-scale production since the metal cannot be tapped off as it forms. The bowl has to be broken open to get the smelted metal out. Other forms of furnace in dome and shaft shapes were developed. These have tapping holes at the base so that the metal can be removed without breaking the furnace. They are recharged with layers of ore and fuel, giving a more efficient use of heat than bowl furnaces. Copper ores reduce to metal at about 1100°C.

Charcoal derived from wood is one of the best fuels for providing a steady temperature and is used for smelting non-ferrous and ferrous metals. In central Asia coke or dried coal was also used.

After smelting the resulting metal is often re-melted in a crucible or deep container, which needs tongs to handle it. The molten metal is then cast by pouring it into a mould to form an ingot. The ingot may then be forged or hammered into the shape required. Non-ferrous metals are forged either hot or cold. Copper quickly cracks if it is hammered, so it is often alloyed with other metals to give it different properties. Alloying metals also lowers the melting point which is required during smelting, making the metal easier to work.

An alloy of copper and tin produces bronze. The proportions vary depending on the purpose of production. A mixture of about 90 per cent copper and 10 per cent tin gives a hard bronze suitable for weapons; 20 per cent tin gives an alloy suitable for bell casting. This tin content produces a metal which can be forged red-hot but is malleable when quenched or cooled quickly by plunging into cold water. An alloy of 30 per cent tin gives speculum metal, which is white and suitable for mirrors, whilst a 3 per cent tin content may be used for coinage.

Brass is produced by alloying copper and zinc. Again the proportions vary, ranging between 60 and 90 per cent copper and between 10 and 40 per cent zinc, depending on the finished products. A 40 per cent zinc content is used when brass is to be cast. Many Tibetan and Islamic metalwares, which are often referred to as 'bronzes', are in fact made from brass.

After being cast, copper and its alloys may be hammered into sheet metal. If they are hammered too much they become brittle and liable to crack. To overcome this the metal is annealed or reheated to dull red and allowed to cool. This softens the metal and further hammering can occur without cracking. Annealing may be repeated several times if extensive hammering is needed. Sheet metal produced in this way is used to make both figures and domestic utensils in central Asia.

Ingots may also be re-melted and shaped by pouring molten

metal into a variety of pre-shaped moulds. *Open moulds* have a shaped depression in stone, clay or metal. They are used to cast solid objects: knife or axe blades, spearheads and coin blanks. *Piece moulds* are made from two or more shaped pieces fitted together. The junction of the pieces usually leaves a 'flash' mark on the object, a sure sign of piece moulding if not removed after casting. Ritual thunderbolts are made in this way in Mongolia and Tibet. *Sand casting* is used to produce small solid objects such as figures or belt plaques, or parts of larger objects which are then joined or welded together. A moulding box in two halves is packed with fine sand and earth, which is then impressed with the pattern of the object required. The pattern or model is removed, the two halves of the mould are put together and molten metal is poured in. After cooling, the moulded piece is usually finished by smoothing or filing. Tibetan bells are made by this method.

Other types of moulds are used to produce hollow figures, tools with sockets and vessels. Moulding may be done around a *false core*, often of clay, which is inserted into the mould to produce a socketed tool or weapon.

Lost-wax or *cire perdue* casting is an ancient technique practised in many parts of the world. The famous 'flying horses' made by the Chinese two thousand years ago, which represented the horses of Sogdiana, were formed by this method. In central Asia many Buddhist figures were made in this way, as they are for the tourist market today. A wax model is formed over a clay core, then covered with an outer layer of clay, which is allowed to dry. The wax and its 'sandwich' of clay layers are heated to melt the wax away through holes in the outer layer of clay. Molten metal is then poured into the clay mould. After cooling, the outer layer of clay is broken to retrieve the metal object. The inner clay core may be left in place or raked out, and the cast object finished by filing and smoothing. A major cause of failure in lost-wax casting is 'gassing', when gas fumes from the molten metal block its free flow through the mould. A good supply of beeswax is needed for this method of production.

Once cast or formed into sheet metal, non-ferrous and precious metals are shaped by various methods:

Sinking: the metal is hammered into a depression on an anvil to form a bowl or cup shape.
Raising: the metal is hammered from the outside over a dome-shaped stake anvil.

43. A silversmith and his wares; Lhasa, Tibet; 1920s. (Pitt Rivers Museum.)

Forming: thin sheet or metal foil is shaped by pressing it over a former made from wood, clay or metal.

Wire drawing: rods of metal are drawn through progressively smaller holes in an iron plate. This method is used to produce decorative wire of gold and silver for jewellery.

Sheet metal and cast sections joined with solder or rivets form a completed figure or vessel. Soldering, the joining of metals with solder, an alloy that has a low melting point (lead and tin are often used), is done by two methods: soft soldering and hard soldering or brazing. In soft soldering the solder is applied at below red-hot temperatures to the keyed metal sections. This method gives weak joints. In hard soldering a molten filler alloy, often of copper and zinc, is used at above red heat to fill and join sections of metal more strongly.

Both Islamic and Buddhist wares provide examples of these methods of metalworking. Large Buddhist figures in Tibet and Mongolia were often made by a combination of working methods, the head and hands being cast separately and the body and limbs made from sheet. The parts were then joined by pins or rivets and soldering. The foundries of Dolon-Nor in Mongolia produced bronze and brass bells, figures and religious utensils for all the Buddhist areas of central Asia. When visited by Huc and

Gabet in 1844, they had just produced a huge statue for the Dalai Lama. The figure, cast in sections, was packed on six camels for transport to Lhasa, where the sections were soldered together.

Foundry techniques and the tools used for working non-ferrous metals have changed little since the bronze age, although the development of iron tools made metalworking easier. A smith needs a forge, anvils, hammers, tongs, punches, chisels and saws. Snips for cutting metal are a relatively recent invention, as is sand casting.

Mongolian and Tibetan silversmiths have a tool kit similar to that of a European jeweller (figure 43). A Mongolian jeweller's workshop takes up so little space that, set up in one half of a tent, it allows domestic life to continue during production (figure 44).

Ironworking

Ironworking requires several techniques different from those used in working non-ferrous and precious metals. During smelting, oxygen must be excluded to prevent the ore re-oxidising. Limestone may be added as a flux to help separate the iron from the slag and make smelting more economical. Iron ores reduce to metal between 1100 and 1500°C, depending on their purity.

44. Interior of a metalworker's tent, with Buddhist figures in process of manufacture; Ulan Bator, Mongolian People's Republic; 1979.

The result of smelting iron ore is a 'bloom', or grey, spongy mass of iron nodules mixed with clay and slag. This needs repeated reheating and hammering to remove the waste and produce recognisable, workable iron.

Iron must be transformed into steel to make useful weapons, armour and tools, which were the primary products before the twentieth century. Iron may also be alloyed with other metals. In Fergana over two thousand years ago the Chinese extracted uranium ore and alloyed it with iron to make picks. These examples are not common and steel is most frequently used. Steel is iron which has absorbed carbon. It is produced by placing the iron in a forge and covering it with burning charcoal for several hours. The charcoal is replenished and bellows used as necessary during this process.

Steel is much harder and more brittle than iron but its qualities can be altered in various ways. If steel is reheated and then allowed to cool slowly by being buried in sand or ashes, a softer, tougher and more flexible metal is produced. Neither steel nor iron can be softened by rapid quenching like copper. If hot steel is cooled rapidly by quenching it in cold water, a hard brittle metal useful for chisels and weapons is produced.

Iron and steel must be worked or forged into shape while they are hot, so tongs are an essential part of a smith's tool kit. Forging often results in decorative effects as the two metals are welded or joined together during hammering.

Apart from being hammered into shape, iron may be cast into moulds while it is molten. Casting iron was a particular feature of Chinese metalworking after ironworking developed there from about 700 BC, whereas in Europe cast iron was rare until about AD 1300. Cast iron is too brittle for making weapons and it was not until suitable bellows had been developed about 200 BC that the Chinese could produce a tougher iron suitable for weapons. The nomadic peoples of central Asia may have invented this double-action piston bellows as well as transmitting ironworking skills across the region.

6
Museums

United Kingdom

British Museum, Great Russell Street, London WC1B 3DG. Telephone: 071-636 1555.

Horniman Museum and Library, London Road, Forest Hill, London SE23 3PQ. Telephone: 081-699 1872, 2339 or 4911.

Manchester Museum, The University of Manchester, Oxford Road, Manchester M13 9PL. Telephone: 061-275 2634.

Museum of Mankind (The Ethnography Department of the British Museum), 6 Burlington Gardens, London W1X 2EX. Telephone: 071-323 8043.

Pitt Rivers Museum, South Parks Road, Oxford OX1 3PP. Telephone: 0865 270927.

Royal Museum of Scotland, Chambers Street, Edinburgh EH1 1JF. Telephone: 031-225 7534.

Victoria and Albert Museum, Cromwell Road, South Kensington, London SW7 2RL. Telephone: 071-938 8500.

Whitworth Art Gallery, The University of Manchester, Oxford Road, Manchester M15 6ER. Telephone: 061-273 4865.

China

Cultural Palace of the Minorities, Fu Xing Men Nei Da Je, Beijing.

Denmark

Nationalmuseet, Ny Vestergade 10, DK-1471 Copenhagen K.

France

Musée de l'Homme, Palais de Chaillot, Place du Trocadéro, 75016 Paris.

Musée Guimet, 6 Place d'Iéna, 75016 Paris.

Germany

Linden Museum of Ethnology, Hegelplatz 1, 7000 Stuttgart, Baden-Württemberg.

Museum für Völkerkunde, Arnimallee 23-27, 1000 Berlin 33.

Museum für Völkerkunde, Taubchenweg 2, 701 Leipzig.

Museum of Indian Art, Takustrasse 40, 1000 Berlin 33.

Museum of Oriental Art, Universitätstrasse 100, 5000 Cologne, Nordrhein-Westfalen.

India
Anthropology Department Museum, Department of Anthropology, University of Delhi, New Delhi 7.
National Museum of India, Janpath, New Delhi 11.
Tibet House Museum, 16 Jor Bagh, New Delhi.

Netherlands
Rijksmuseum voor Volkenkunde, Steenstraat 1, 2300 AE Leiden, Zuid Holland.

Sweden
Ethnographical Museum of Sweden, Djurgardsbrunnsvägen 34, 5-115 27 Stockholm.

Turkey
Topkapi Palace Museum, Istanbul.

USSR
A. Ikramov State Museum of the History of Culture and Art, Sovetskaya ul 51, Samarkand, Uzbek SSR.
Historical and Ethnographical Museum of Bukhara, Bukhara, Uzbek SSR.
Museum of the Republic of Tadzhikstan, Lenina, Dushanbe, Tadzhik SSR.
Omsk District Museum, Omsk, West Siberia, RSFSR.
State Hermitage Museum, M. Dvortsovaya Naberezhnaya, Leningrad.
State Historical Museum of the Kirghiz, Krasnooktyabrskaya, Frunze, Kirghiz SSR.
State Museum of Oriental Art, Ul Obukha 16, Moscow.
Tashkent Central Regional Museum, Tashkent, Uzbek SSR.

United States of America
Asian Art Museum of San Francisco, Golden Gate Park, San Francisco, California 94118.
Jacques Marchais Center of Tibetan Arts, 338 Lighthouse Avenue, Staten Island, New York 10306.
Los Angeles County Museum of Art, 5905 Wilshire Boulevard, Los Angeles, California 90036.
Metropolitan Museum of Art, 5th Avenue at 82nd Street, New York, NY 10028.
The Newark Museum, 49 Washington Street, Newark, New Jersey 07101.

7
Further reading

Bacon, E. E. *Central Asians under Russian Rule*. Cornell University Press, London, 1980.

Bamborough, P. *Treasures of Islam*. Blandford Press, Poole, 1976.

Barthold, W. *Turkestan down to the Mongol Invasion*. Luzac, Thetford, 1977.

Bell, Sir Charles. *The People of Tibet*. Oxford University Press, Oxford, 1928.

Bowles, G. T. *The People of Asia*. Weidenfeld and Nicolson, London, 1977.

Boyer, M. *Mongol Jewellery*. Nationalmuseets Skrifter, Etnografisk Roekke v, Copenhagen, 1980.

British Museum. *Frozen Tombs. The Culture and Art of the Ancient Tribes of Siberia*. British Museum Publications, London, 1978.

Denwood, P. (editor). *Arts of the Eurasian Steppelands*. Colloquy 7, Percival David Foundation, London, 1978.

Eberhard, W. *A History of China*. Routledge Kegan Paul, London, 1977.

Family of Man (number 57). Articles on the Khalkha, Kazakhs and Uzbeks. Marshall Cavendish, 1975.

Frankel, D. *Metalwork in Ancient Western Asia*. British Museum Publications, London, 1977.

Hodges, H. *Artifacts*. John Baker, London, 1964.

Hodges, H. *Technology in the Ancient World*. Penguin, Harmondsworth, 1970.

Jagchid, S. and Hyer, P. *Mongolia's Culture and Society*. Dawson, Folkestone, 1979.

Jasiewicz, Z. 'Traditional Handicrafts of Uzbekistan in the Process of Culture Changes in the Second Half of the Nineteenth and in the Twentieth Centuries', *Ethnologia Polona*, volume 3 (1977).

Kalter, J. *Arts and Crafts of Turkestan*. Thames and Hudson, London, 1984.

Lattimore, O. *Inner Asian Frontiers of China*. Beacon Press, Boston, 1962.

Lattimore, O. *Desert Road to Turkestan*. AMS Press, London, 1972.

MacDonald, D. *Cultural Heritage of Tibet*. Light and Life, New

Delhi, undated.

Mongait, A. L. *Archaeology in the USSR*. Penguin, Harmondsworth, 1961.

Morgan, D. *The Mongols*. Basil Blackwell, Oxford, 1986.

Osborne, H. (editor). *Oxford Companion to the Decorative Arts*. Oxford University Press, Oxford, 1985.

Philipps, E. D. *The Royal Hordes*. Thames and Hudson, London, 1965.

Rawson, J. *Chinese Ornament, the Lotus and the Dragon*. British Museum Publications, London, 1984.

Rice, D. T. *Islamic Art*. Thames and Hudson, London, 1977.

Rice, T. T. *The Scythians*. Praeger, New York, 1957.

Rice, T. T. *The Ancient Arts of Central Asia*. Thames and Hudson, London, 1965.

Robinson, B. 'Metalwork', in *The Arts of Islam*. Arts Council, London, 1976.

Simkin, C. G. F. *The Traditional Trade of Asia*. Oxford University Press, London, 1968.

Snellgrove, D. and Richardson, H. *A Cultural History of Tibet*. Weidenfeld and Nicolson, London, 1968.

Stein, R. A. *Tibetan Civilisation*. Faber and Faber, London, 1972.

Tucci, G. *Tibet, Land of Snows*. Elek, London, 1967.

Tucci, G. *Transhimalaya*. Barrie and Jenkins, London, 1973.

Vainshtein, S. *Nomads of South Siberia*. Cambridge University Press, London, 1980.

Watson, W. *Style in the Arts of China*. Universe, New York, 1974.

Wulff, H. E. *Traditional Crafts of Persia*. Massachusetts Institute of Technology, Cambridge, Massachusetts, 1966.

Zwalf, W. *Heritage of Tibet*. British Museum Publications, London, 1981.

64

Index

Page numbers in italic refer to illustrations.